Your
Disappearance

Todd,
Hope you like it!

David Wirthlin

BlazeVOX [books]

Buffalo, New York

Your Disappearance by David Wirthlin

Copyright © 2009

Published by BlazeVOX [books]

Printed in the United States of America

Book design by Geoffrey Gatza

First Edition
ISBN: 9781935402404
Library of Congress Control Number 2009925616

BlazeVOX [books]
14 Tremaine Ave
Kenmore, NY 14217

Editor@blazevox.org

publisher of weird little books

BlazeVOX [books]

blazevox.org

2   4   6   8   0   9   7   5   3   1

B   X

Acknowledgments

Portions of this work have previously been published in The 2nd Hand, Sleepingfish, Denver Quarterly, and elimae.

Achilles absent, was Achilles still.

-Homer

Contents

Your Disappearance

Rod is Canaries

Everyday I wake up thinking about her. Those bare feet on cold asphalt. To anyone else this is trivial. To me, to her, all encompassing, important. Kids running in the night, the night running the kids. The writing on the asphalt in wax. Shuffle shuffle feet, bare and cold, roughed up in the middle of the night. I wonder how any of this happened, speculate if it did.

Again, the writing on the asphalt, Rod is Canaries.

Who did this? Don't know.

You? Course not.

How any of this means, the subjectivity of Rod being canaries.

The kid walks like a giraffe, arm braces up front, standard human biped in back, head pointed up, neck stretched, straining. Quadruped instead of winged.

Maybe he did it.

The kid can't even talk, how could he write?

Considering the nature of a person predisposed to obsession.

Morning after the cold night, she called, What is Rod is Canaries?

I give up, what is it? Give me the punch line.

I am the punch line.

Use me interchangeably with her and me. Run simultaneously with Rod is Canaries.

What is the limit, the threshold before a spiral? The writing outside never washed away. Scrubbing all night, into the morning, giraffes lacking the ability to arrange words, the impossibility of relating to handicaps. She could never address it directly, but confronted it daily.

In the park, reading a book, bare feet on the cold asphalt. Violet sky, purple sky, always resting on the bench.

Clik clak clik clak.

How could anyone do this to him? Indirectly to me?

Clik clak clik clak, coming closer.

Purple sky shifting back to violet, absorbed in a book, but hearing.

Clik clak clik clak, almost upon her.

I never imagined my mornings like this.

How did you get here?

Clik clak.

Does Mom know?

Clik clak, right upon her.

Arm braces fall off, clak clak on the ground. Giraffe, he stands erect, leaps in the air, hovers. Blue ball of light envelops Rod, growing larger, brighter, exploding. Beams of light outward, dissipating in the violet sky. A canary hovers above, gently flapping wings. Lands on her head, tugging at hair. Pecking at her head, beak full of hair, pecking at her head, beak full of skull, pecking at her head, beak full of brain.

Had we known all this, all this would be averted. Everyday like this without fail.

I can't understand it. What is to understand? It's everyday. Me too.

Can the asphalt, cold and rough, hold anything? How do we look without looking? In the time that has passed, has there been any indication of this?

We will run, sit, ponder, cry. Her nights without end are happening now. Mornings try to cover a semblance of memory. In this end we are together, but there, always apart.

The bottom of those feet are worn without reason. Habitual stockyards of asphalt and canaries, time honored, resisted.

Will it never end? But we cannot. Of course.

Before cold asphalt was smiles and warmth. But nevertheless sinister.

Is there ever such thing as really letting go?

In front of the house, the writing. If this only had been important to you.

Clik clak clik clak.

I will conjure her at any point, if necessary.

Clik clak clik clak.

Please.

Stop.

Arm braces drop, triumphant. In the sky, above her head, hovering, bright blue, Rod, the ball of blue, expands, bursts. Canaries canaries canaries, swirling, diving, everywhere. Canaries canaries canaries, flecks of skull, bits of brain, blood.

This can only end at no end. And yet, only she, not I, and I, not she. Interchangeably, not interlocking.

The very nature of us, him, her, I. Back to the night, after one revolution, waking to it every morning.

I cannot handle another time.

Rod is canaries, regardless.

My view of the house unblemished by wax. The approach of bare feet on grass.

Swoosh swoosh swoosh.

Listen to what I've heard.

Smoke billows out of her mouth, and a light in her throat grows brighter. The tracks extend to the tip of her tongue. At the tip of the tracks the train spills out of her mouth into a viscous puddle on the floor.

Of all the places for this to happen, of all the times, of all.

Swoosh swoosh swoosh.

She floats, a ball of blue that explodes into hundreds of yellow birds. Pecking at me, at herself.

Number One

These pencil shavings are immersive and I struggle to breath. My eyes aren't open but I know I'm in a box. All around me - up, down, side to side. These pencil shavings are not an accident. The box is a five-foot square, completely full of shavings. I'm a part of this, and the pencil shavings spill over. The floor piles are contaminated and can't be used.

Saxophonist

A man plays a saxophone along the banks of a concrete riverbed. He is the only person within a hundred yard radius, and he plays facing a wall. From our standpoint, we can't hear any sound, so it's only an assumption that he actually plays. The thought crossed your mind that it would be wonderful if he wasn't playing. He was a saxophone mime without an audience, a performer at heart but musically talentless. He was an introvert, you said, a claustrophobic introvert that could not remain in that little apartment of his. His ex-wife was agoraphobic, and this irreconcilable difference ultimately led to their undoing.

A Future Event

We liked to sound smart,

We kept going back and forth on your idea of futurism, often in heated debate. The future is now, you always started with, and at which point I rolled my eyes. We are living in the future of the past. There is never a now, only a future now. When I make a statement, the time that elapses from word utterance to sound recognition and then brain computation, though slight, roots those instances in two separate times. As such, I know that when I make a statement, I know it's only existence is in a future time. Everything is always either past or future. There is no present.

I always responded by commenting on how ridiculous you could be. Time is more complicated than two mere divisions. You mention the past and the future, but where is the division between the two? There must be some separation, even if only a flash or a blip, there is a line that divides, and that line is the present.

Why must there be a dividing line? In reality there is only one continuous time. We create divisions in time for our own clarity, but time is always moving. Both past and present are static. Only the future moves.

The future only moves because the present pushes it forward. You're right when you say time is continuous, but your focus is off. The past and the future are imaginary constructs, and we are always grounded in the reality of the present. As the present moves rapidly along, we move along with it, and the construct of the future is constantly pushed out of our reach.

You threw the lamp at me and I jumped out of the way.

If you are so sure that the future is unattainable, why were your actions motivated by a future event? You only jumped out of the way because of the danger of getting hit by the lamp, a future event.

You threw a lamp at me.
To prove a point.
You threw a lamp at me.

but we were both so incredibly stupid.

Lemon

You had that lemon seed stuck in your nostril. At night, you picked at it until blood trickled out. You imagined the blood would lubricate the seed and the flow would move it along, but it continued to plague you into the morning. You awakened with blood crusted on the rim of your nose and on your pillow. Every day in the shower you blew your nose into your hands, and the seed would slip between your fingers, bounce on the shower floor and disappear down the drain.

Pieces of Unequal Stories

Small mass,

Die frivolous and disgraceful, curt and foolish.

Cysts are only curt stories of the past, and they die a genius of small bags. When fingers die, they are only curt stories of the past, and a fragment of small bags, no less. Mischievous stories are often unequal and broken, the fragment of pettiness put together and broken up, windows of minuteness into a disgraceful mass. The pieces of unequal stories are broken up into a foolish past. They are windows into the minuteness of genius, and the genius of a fragment. The mischievous pieces never die, and they are often broken into fingers.

Your Dogs

One of the dogs has its jaw wired shut, with only a
small opening on one side for breathing, eating,
drinking. Mostly, its tongue hangs out. It walks up to
me and lays down, head on my bag. Water drips off the
jowls; the tongue goes in and out trying to catch the
water, but instead, saliva pools on the edge of the
opening until it is thick and white. It has difficulty
breathing through the small opening, and the harder it
breathes, the heavier the saliva pool gets. Finally, the
saliva slides off the edge of the opening slowly, and the
droplet barely hangs on. It drops onto my bag, then
slides onto my foot. I look around to see if anyone else
has noticed, but no one gives any indication they have.
The other dog is blind, its eyes aqua and milky, its coat
milky too. It lumbers into the room, knocks into a
chair, heads straight toward me. It's not slowing down

and it's only a few feet away; then inches from me and the other dog, it stops, sits, stares. Those aqua eyes penetrate me. I know it's not really staring, because it can't, but it's unnerving. I wonder what a completely blind dog does when it directs its eyes at someone. It can't know it's looking at me, and yet, for the remainder of my time here, it never breaks that gaze.

Number Two

The rock has been polished to a remarkable sheen - a lustrous and dripping mirrored finish. The kind of rock that is slippery when wet and even more so when dry. Flip it over in my pocket once. I remove my hand and the rock turns perpetually. The gleaming rock could make teeth chatter in the winter. But this is summer, so it just spins in my pocket.

Iron Rich Fertility

The bones rise up, separate, hover around you, and now you are in the midst of bones. You lie with your back in the mud dense with iron rich fertility. Foliage breaks the surface of the mud around you, little green fingers emerging from brown, bones hovering above you. The foliage reaches for bones, and all you do is watch as green arms extend skyward, surrounding you. At first, the plants are cold to the touch but warm quickly as they wrap tighter. You don't struggle to move or break free; you enjoy this moment, wearing nothing but green. As the plants envelope your entire body, you feel safe, secure. Your smile and dilated pupils are the only things exposed, absorbing the masterpiece I orchestrate from above. Plants grab bones and pull them down gently until they lie around but not on top of you. You see me in the branches of the tree above, and we laugh until our eyes tear up.

The Apple Fell

She took a few steps toward me, then stopped and retreated. She said, What do you think you're doing?

Mostly, I hover upright, like I'm standing, but really I'm not even touching the ground. Sleep-wise, I float horizontal.

Both my teacher and I waited, unwilling to breathe. Most of my classmates looked at our teacher, their eyes pleading for guidance. One student looked toward the ceiling as his legs began to twitch. He looked at me with a smile. My teacher rushed over and handed him a textbook. Will you please hand this to your colleague?

He nodded his head and stood up. His eyes were fixed on the book. Shuffling his feet, he made his way through the maze of desks to where I was hovering. Without making eye contact, he extended the book to me. Sorry, he said.

As soon as the book was in my hands I began drifting down toward my chair. I stopped a couple feet above it. My teacher dug in her bag and produced several other textbooks. She stuffed them in my backpack, and said, Take a look at these, and then tell me what you think. She handed it to me, smirking.

I put the backpack on and plummeted earthward. I bounced off the top of my desk and landed face first on the linoleum floor. My classmates laughed. I remained there until every single person had left the room. All day I wore that bag, and all day I remained grounded.

My Dad punched me in the face, knocking me to my feet. I saw his heart pumping -- his face a red balloon, full of too much air. The school called, he said. What in hell's name do you think you're doing?

I stood erect, blood trickling down my face. We stared at each other forever.   Answer me.

My mouth remained closed.
          Don't think I won't hit you again.
Slowly, I lifted off the ground. He came after me, swinging wildly, but I rose above his punches. Obscenities flew out of his mouth, but those missed me too. He ran to the kitchen, returning with a broom. He painted giant arcs with it, but each time the broom came near the preceding rush of air would shift me out of its path.

He flung the broom against the wall. I could hear tears spilling down his cheeks. I don't get it, he said and sat down on the cold tile floor, his face buried between his knees. He spoke softly to himself, like I no longer existed.

I looked down upon him for several minutes, unsure how to react.

My mother entered the room, scowling and shaking her head. Come with me, she said. She led the way to my bedroom. After a few feet she stopped. Without looking at me, she pointed down and said, On the ground, I quickly obeyed, entering the bedroom on foot. We sat down on my bed. You're killing your father, she said.

I picked at my fingernails. Get some sleep, she said.

When everyone was asleep, I hovered into the kitchen and took out a bottle of my parent's favorite vodka. I filled all the shot glasses my parents owned, and lined them atop the refrigerator.

I woke up plastered to the linoleum floor a few hours

later, breathing urine. Eventually I got up and walked to my room. Walked because I had to. Alcohol and gravity are twins. I found my bed and collapsed.

At school the next day I wore a full backpack. In every class I added a book to ensure I remained grounded. As the day wore on, the pack's effectiveness wore off. I continued adding books until the bottom finally tore out.

I'm a baby again. My mother cradles me in her arms, softly humming a lullaby. She lightly rubs my cheek as she rocks me back and forth. She says, You can do anything you want when you grow up. Anything.

Number Three

I've been wearing this eyelash for days.
But it has not illuminated your vision.
How it affected the original owner, we may never
know.

Consider the Loss

Fragile, like an orchid floating in milk, your grandmother told stories. To think that a woman now so frail, so gentle, could be capable of anything of that magnitude.

There is a peace about her now that I wish you could be here to see. She speaks of you as though you are a distant memory, but you are not far removed. It is clear things requiring forgiveness remain unforgiven.

Consider the loss. These stories fall from your grandmother's tongue while others drip from ours, and all the while you sit unreachable, of your own accord or of necessity. Still, the loss is immeasurable.

Unforgiven, fragile like your grandmother, only strong

in your own versions of the past.

Bare Foot

I still slide my feet, wear socks on the hardwood at night. You hated my bare feet slapping, especially when trying to sleep.

You sat up straight looking disoriented, then upset. Shhhh, you said louder than my bare foot slap. I let it go. Said, Okay.

Tried to just slide or shuffle, but bare feet don't slide, and squeak when shuffling. Slippers are cumbersome and loud.

You never woke during my experimentation period, but did stir. Eventually found socks worked best. Silent and slippery, but impossible to sleep in.

Kept a pair next to the night stand, put them on every time I woke up needing a drink or a trip to the bathroom, took them off before getting back in bed.

How many times do I have to ask you to put your socks away? Sorry. I'll try to do better. Just put them in your drawer. I'll try, okay?

But the drawer is too loud and too far way. Too much risk of waking you. Much rather be the slob and let you sleep than give it away.

You never knew any of this because it worked. Though the house is empty, I put socks on every time I crawl out of bed, sometimes out of habit, others because I feel you're there, like I might wake you, even if I know I can't.

Number Four

9:06:14 FS Melbourne, this is Delta Sierra Juliet. Is
there any known traffic below five
thousand?'

9:06:23 Delta Sierra Juliet—No known traffic.

9:06:26 I am—seems (to) be a large aircraft below 5,000.

9:06:46 Delta Sierra Juliet—What type of aircraft is it?

9:06:50 I cannot affirm. It is four bright … it seems to
me like landing lights.

9:07:04 Delta Sierra Juliet. [This statement affirms
to the pilot that the person on the ground
heard his transmission.]

9:07:32 FS Melbourne, this (is) Delta Sierra Juliet. The aircraft has just passed over me at least a thousand feet above.

9:07:43 Delta Sierra Juliet—Roger—and it, it is a large aircraft—confirm?

9:07:47 Er, unknown due to the speed it's travelling... is there any airforce aircraft in the vicinity?

9:07:57 Delta Sierra Juliet. No known aircraft in the vicinity.

9:08:18 FS Melbourne... it's approaching now from due east~ towards me.~

9:08:28 Delta Sierra Juliet.

9:08:42 //Open microphone for two seconds//

9:08:49 It seems to me that he's playing some sort of game.'—He's flying over me two—three times at a time at speeds I could not identify.'

9:09:02 Delta Sierra Juliet—Roger. What is your actual level?

9:09:06 My level is four and a half thousand, four five zero zero.~

9:09:11 Delta Sierra Juliet... And confirm—you cannot identify the aircraft.

9:09:14 Affirmative.

9:09:18 Delta Sierra Juliet—Roger... standby.

9:09:28 FS Melbourne, It's not an aircraft'... it is //open microphone for two seconds//

9:09:46 Delta Sierra Juliet—Melbourne. Can you describe the...er—aircraft?

9:09:52 ...as it's flying past it's a long shape' //open microphone for three seconds // (cannot) identify more than that. It has such speed //open microphone for three seconds //. It is before me right now Melbourne.'

9:10:07 Delta Sierra Juliet—Roger. And how large would the —er—object be?

9:10:20 DSJ FS Delta Sierra Juliet—Melbourne. It seems like it's (stationary). What I'm doing right now is orbiting, and the thing is just orbiting on top of me also' ... It's got a green light,' and sort of metallic (like)~. It's all shiny (on) the outside.

9:10:43 Delta Sierra Juliet.

9:10:48 It's just vanished.

9:10:57 Delta Sierra Juliet.

9:11:03 FS Melbourne would you know what kind
of aircraft I've got?' It is military aircraft?'

9:11:08 Delta Sierra Juliet. Confirm the... er—aircraft
just vanished.

9:11:14 Say again.

9:11:17 Delta Sierra Juliet. Is the aircraft still with you?'

9:11:23... It's ah... Nor //open microphone for two
seconds// (now) approaching from the
southwest.

9:11:37 Delta Sierra Juliet

9:11:52 The engine is, is rough idling. —I've got it set at twenty three—twenty four… and the thing is—coughing.

9:12:04 Delta Sierra Juliet—Roger. What are your intentions?

9:12:09 My intentions are—ah… to go to King Island—Ah, Melbourne, that strange aircraft is hovering on top of me again //open microphone for two seconds// it is hovering and it's not an aircraft.

9:12:22 Delta Sierra Juliet.

9:12:28 FS Melbourne //open microphone for 17 seconds// [A very strange pulsed noise is also audible during this transmission.]

9:12:49 Delta Sierra Juliet.

Car, Drive Through My Open Mouth, Down My Throat

Mostly I shrug when I hear, How do you feel? How are you doing? or whatever I get asked, because mostly I don't know because the answer shifts so much. I usually don't make the effort to pinpoint it. If I gave an answer, by the time the answer actually formed in my head, then by the time it came out, I would be feeling something else. So why bother if what I say isn't even accurate?

You're probably hoping I'll take a stab at it anyway. You're curious maybe, or concerned. Why not? What's the harm? you offer. You want me to get in touch with the moment, I guess, or help you get in touch with my moment. Of course it's easier not to, you say. I know this is hard. Sometimes the only way is the hard way. The only right way.

You're right, but after I offer this, I won't even be feeling it. I might as well be making this up, because what I felt when I said it, and what I feel now, or even what I'll feel later, are not the same as what I said in the first place. You understand that right? Maybe there's no harm, maybe it's better for me, but what use is it to you if it's not even what I feel?

We could, perhaps, dispense with these formalities. If you ask just to ask, I'll answer just to answer. How does this help anyone? Of course, you insist, so I oblige.

I feel like a car has driven through my open mouth, down my throat, and now rests somewhere in my bowels. As much as that hurts, I know it'll hurt worse later because somehow I've got to figure a way to excrete it.

Your Grandmother

Your grandmother stares at me too, like the dog with milky blind eyes. Even with her cataracts and thick glasses, she watches my every move. As she sits telling stories to the group, she stares.

She stares as though she's really just telling the stories to me. They don't seem to have relevance, but her stare gives them relevance; the longer she stares, the more they gain in relevance, and the more they gain in relevance, the harder she seems to stare.

No one asks her to tell the stories, she just does, always has when people are together. She usually spreads her penetrating gaze throughout the group, but not this time.

Between stories, I stand up, walk to the kitchen. The blind dog follows. Your grandmother stays seated but follows with her eyes until I round the corner. Even after I'm out of her sight line, I feel like she's watching me through the wall, like the blind dog is a homing device, so she always knows where I am.

I try to sneak a peek by looking at her reflection in the mirror, and her eyes meet mine on that two dimensional plane. What am I supposed to do with this? Try to makes heads or tails of it, or ignore it? She's old, and only lucid when telling stories, and then only partially so. Or is that just an easy way to explain it away? If I ignore it, will she eventually stop?

I walk out the kitchen door, to the side of the house, making sure the dog doesn't follow, open the side gate, walk down the street.

Number Five

A box arrives on the doorstep addressed to you, return address from you. After considering the legal ramifications for some time, I finally open it, only to find it empty except for a barely legible note scrawled on a receipt. I'm sorry. I couldn't take this box anymore. I had to leave, it said.

The Terms of Your Disappearance

I sometimes get confused about what constitutes your disappearance. It seems something present, when a disappearance occurs, loses presence, but really, it doesn't. It adjusts to occupy new space, an often unknown space.

The terms of your disappearance are always shifting, like my feelings about it are always shifting, leaving a pool of uneasy definitions and disappointing confusion. Disappearance in the general sense I typically assume - something once present, now absent - is really a form of transformation.

In its transformation to a butterfly, couldn't it be said the caterpillar - what we know as a caterpillar -

disappears? If we're talking about disappearance and vanishing in the same vein, aren't they just instances of transforming materiality to immateriality or material to invisible material?

So when I talk of your disappearance, am I limited to material transformation? Is that what happened? You were here, but now you are not? You are here though, if only in memory form, you are here. You occupy mental space, which is physical.

Does the fact I cannot see you limit your presence? This presence alters my actions, thoughts, future. I cannot touch you any longer. When I speak, you no longer respond. If you were here, if I could brush your hair behind your ear with my fingers, and I spoke, but you didn't respond, like the last time you were here, could we say you had already disappeared, transformed emotionally, if not in physical totality?

Where do I look to pinpoint your disappearance? The physical absence or much sooner, when you had presence in the flesh, but only in a lessened state, a physicality nearing absence? Or did you disappear when the spiral first started? Is this created by me?

Could we still be in that process, and will only be complete when this stops, only when I stop thinking, pondering, crying, lamenting your disappearance in whatever form that may be? The transformation to disappearance only stops, the disappearance complete, when this stops?

Haiku Abating

I.

She squats to pee next to a clump of trees.

I stand a short distance away, out of sight.

A mob of kangaroos huddles on the other side of the
clump of trees. One of them, I suppose the leader, hops
over to her. She stands up, startled.

Face to face with the kangaroo now, shoulders slumped
submissively. The kangaroo literally looks like it wants
to box.

She starts talking. What I presume to be talking. I'm
close enough to hear, but can't. Her mouth moves in the

manner of talking. Hands gesture to accompany speech, but again, no sound.

As soon she starts this talk-like manner, the kangaroo becomes subdued. The more animated she is, the more lethargic the kangaroo.

This continues for several minutes.

I think, The kangaroo looks like it will die any second.

The kangaroo drops to the ground, breathing heavy at first, foam collecting at the corners of her mouth. Breathing slows until it finally stops.

She doesn't stick around to see it die, but I can verify it.

Whether her doing or mine, the kangaroo is dead, and she will suffer for it.

II.

She has been in her cell for some thirteen years. Other than dealing with the guilt for killing that kangaroo, it seems her life in prison is not too bad.

Her cell is a comfortable six by eight feet, and she has all the amenities she needs.

The cell is conveniently made of limestone, which can decompose a human body in six months.

When she dies, they'll board up her window and door. In six months, a little vacuuming, and she'll be gone.

I still can't hear her talk, but I check in from time to time.

To pass time, and to her abate her guilt, she spends nearly all her time writing poems. Here is a sample haiku:

> Oh beautiful 'roo
> I never meant to kill you
> Now I rot in jail

Time is short and her mind is nearly gone, but she's not worried about when it finally goes.

Every day I think about that kangaroo. Sometimes I wish I would lose my mind just to stop thinking about her.

Number Six

When it settles on the roof like this, the ceiling is bound to bleed. While it does drip into the sink occasionally, it mostly likes to remain congealed. This pancake-sized spot of reddish viscosity is not the answer, but maybe the drip in the sink. That drip, floating in tepid water. It's not the drip itself, but what caused the drip, and it's not gravity or time. I scoop up the drip and wrap it in a handkerchief.

Your Grandmother Stares

After a few trips around the block, I return to the kitchen, find the blind dog waiting for me at the door. It follows me back to my seat, and lies down next to your grandmother once I'm seated. There is no one else left in the room, except your grandmother and the two dogs. The dog with it's jaw wired shut shuffles over, lies right next to the blind dog at your grandmother's feet, as though they're guarding her. There is a connection between her and these dogs I don't understand. Grandmother doesn't talk, hardly moves, for several minutes, but continues to stare. The room is silent except for the wired jaw dog lapping saliva off its jowls. We sit like this long enough for the sun to set and the room to get dark. I'm terrified to leave now, but don't know why. She stares like she wants to tell me something, but doesn't, or can't.

My Distance

I sometimes wished for a clean break, but invested enough I felt the need to keep it going.

You see, I often got bored with you. What often seemed like your disappearance was actually my distance.

Bored may not be accurate. More like tired. No, exhausted, and I got so exhausted I lost interest.

I got tired of the constant presence, consistent demand of meeting expectations that may or may not have been realistic, but were certainly more than I wanted to meet.

This isn't the case now is it? I don't have any control this time. Even when I thought I did, I really didn't.

When I created distance, I thought I was exerting control, but it was really just a vain manifestation of my lack thereof.

This time it's not a matter of control, just a spiral, beyond influence.

Fire Shroud

Finally, she moves. Sitting with her arms crossed, she rocks back and forth in her chair, the chair itself not moving. She rocks faster, increasing friction. Then a spark, followed by a small flame. Waves of heat course through her body, traveling from limb to limb. Yellow flames envelope her, growing hotter until a blinding, white fire shrouds her. When the flame dies out, only scorch marks remain. The dogs lick the dark spot where she once sat.

Minute Tatters and Filaments

The cysts, the bags, the genius, are past. When they die, bags and cysts are broken up into minute tatters and filaments, small pieces between the fingers.

Time and genius put together only curt fragments, unequal stories, compartments.

When they die, time and genius are broken up into unequal compartments, small pieces put together between minuteness and a foolish, frivolous, disgraceful past.

Ritual

Five rows of children, ten deep, on a field, all facing the same direction. Each child wears blue shorts and a white t-shirt, except the head of each row wears a yellow shirt.

The children stand motionless for several minutes while parents watch idly from the stands. In unison, the head of each row turns to face the other children.

After a few more minutes of motionless silence, the head children raise their hands and clap, slowly at first, then building frenetically.

The fourth child in row three begins to cry, just momentarily, regains composure and smiles. The head children stop clapping; the other children exhale a long, drawn out breath, and the head of each row combusts in blinding white flames.

As the heads burn, the remaining rows consume themselves in conflagration, all fifty children enveloped in piercing white heat. The parents get up and file out of the bleachers.

Head children are only smoldering heaps of ashes now, and it's not long before the rest are too. Once the parents have left, sprinklers turn on, water dissolves the ash.

The sprinklers turn off, the ashy water recedes, absorbed by the soil, leaving fifty scorch marks in the middle of the field.

Another group of fifty children file onto the field and line up on the scorch marks.

After All This

After she had both breasts mastectomized,

three surgeries to remove cataracts (and refusing a

fourth),

a hip replacement,

a mild stroke,

chronic cysts on her ovaries,

a hysterectomy,

living with a mind not sharp enough to talk about

anything but the past,

your grandmother passed away when an inept medical

practitioner mixed Low-P with her prescriptions at a

level toxic for a women of her diminished physicality.

Context of a Birth

I could be thinking about your physical placement, what can be a continuum and what is chance. You place yourself innately on a mesa. There are blue hills at each horizon, the light falls onto your open space, the path of the sun and the planets are proportioned around you.

My perception of your location is not contingent, but accords with an idea of location inside you, that turns in you like a gyroscope, as you are moving. I believe in this sense perception of place, because you experience it. Your father was away, fighting, the village under attack. The house shook, and your mother was in heavy labor and surrounded by women. She didn't cry, but sat in a puddle of urine and excrement.

By the time the shelling stopped, you'd been bundled and put to your mother's breast. The women stayed around them. It was a matter of debate whether this tiny spirit would remain, when the souls of so many were leaving like a wave that had to be struggled against. It may be a sense of the shape of a space, or of the balance of features of the space, or it may be a sense of a point on the earth in relation to forces in the earth, which may be affected by stars and planets, or it may be in relation to stars and planets. The world is unhinged like that, or at least your mother was.

They took her suggestion in stride, and insisted that she was too young, and told her to look at you, that she had to stay home and help you, that she would be much more useful that way. So she did. So the place would sit in her, its wide space with sun, as what it would be in her memory of this time, how it would be perceived is a matrix of how you were with some people around you, not agents but catalyst or fuel for the perception of light on a wide space, so free as to be impersonal in the company, implacable and impersonal.

Splintered Tongues, Pelts

Your dogs have splintered tongues, grooved jowls from the chair edge. The dark spot gone, seat almost worn to a hole from licking. C'mon, I call to the dogs, but they still lick. I want them as remembrance, want them in my home, hoping to forge a connection, but they refuse to move from your grandmother's chair. C'mon, let's go. I go to the kitchen looking for food, a bribe, but when I return, the dogs proper are gone. They've left their pelts in a heap next to the chair. For my purposes, this works just as well as, if not better than, the whole dogs. Hoist the pelts over my shoulder, and carry them home.

Parm

Today, went to the grocery store, planning to get ingredients to make chicken parmigiana. It took three trips to get what I needed.

First trip, I came out with bread crumbs and sauce. That's it. I knew I needed more items before entering, but just couldn't focus long enough.

Got home, unpacked and realized, I forgot the chicken. I said it out loud. Chicken. So I went back and got chicken.

Pound the chicken flat, dip it in flour, egg, breadcrumbs and throw it in a pan of hot oil. Find comfort in these simple acts.

Once the breadcrumbs are golden brown, take the chicken out and set it in a pan, top it with sauce, and get ready to slide it in the oven.

But there's no cheese. Two trips already, and still no cheese. Make my final trip, get cheese, slap it on the chicken and bake it til bubbly.

I set plates out, serve the chicken. I got out two plates because I made two chicken breasts.

I set a place for you at the table, even though I know you won't, can't show. I set the place, served the chicken, not thinking you couldn't show, just not thinking.

Sat at the table eating the chicken, but staring the whole time at your full plate, wondering how I could possibly have done this, why I've done this to myself again, not enjoying a meal I should have.

Number Seven

A clump of yellow sticks to the doorknob. There's something that causes the stick, but it's not red like you might think. Nor white or blue. Colorless really, and transparent more accurately. Transparency adopts the color of whatever it covers, in this case the doorknob, so the stick this time is brass colored. There's an element of yellow to the stick as well, most likely from the hair, but also possibly from faded brass. The only change after removing the transparency is the loss of stick, which makes the yellow fall.

Low-P

Metallurgists and botanists once argued about the classification of Low-P because of its exceedingly high iron concentration. Metallurgists contend that because it's primarily composed of a metal, it warrants classification as such. The botanist argument is quite clear: Any matter, regardless of physical composition ratios, derived from plant-life, should necessarily be accorded an appropriately botanical classification. What finally put the argument to rest was the discovery of the nature of the iron present in Low-P. That is, the iron in Low-P does not entirely originate in Low-P, and at its inception there is no more remarkable amount present than in any other plant. However, Low-P allows for a high level of absorption of ferromagnetic ore, iron being the most abundantly available. As Low-P absorbs iron, its magnetic field expands and attracts more iron. Low-

P functions as the main activator of seeds which require iron for germination. The most straightforward example of Low-P's role in germination is in the seed of the Xetl tree, which requires comparatively large amounts of iron to germinate. Without Low-P, the seed of the Xetl tree would never grow organically. While the question of classification as a botanical entity has long been answered, metallurgists still keep Low-P on their radar. Some believe Low-P iron absorption, left unabated, could become toxic to the host plant. According to the theory, once the plant matter decays, what's left is thought to condense and solidify as iron ore over time. Thus, Low-P plays an important role in the perpetuation and development of ferromagnetic ore deposits.

Canary at the Cafe

I'm seated on the patio of our favorite cafe, at one of
those round tables for two. It's midmorning on a
weekday and lightly raining, so there's no one walking
the sidewalks, but at least the umbrella is up this time.

The waiter fills my water glass and takes my order. Eggs
Benedict, of course, side of bacon, hash browns. I
almost order your French toast, but catch myself before
it comes out.

A canary lands on the back of the seat opposite mine,
it's yellow feathers wet and ruffled. It cocks its head to
the side, hops from seat to table, hop hops over to my
steaming plate of food, chirps a little, but doesn't sing.
Only the males sing.

I call the waiter over, ask for a second glass of water, and maybe a Belgian waffle, or just one slice of French toast, whichever is easiest. The water comes immediately. It's not sparkling, but I imagine that's better for the canary.

You always waited to drink until after your food was gone. Nothing worse than finishing your meal and have nothing to wash it down with, you said. Even the time you started choking, you wouldn't sip the water to move things along after you caught your breath.

The canary doesn't touch the water, but when the waffle comes, it tears into it, like it hadn't eaten for days, like it might never again. I try to coax it into taking a sip of water, using a straw to place a small drop on the table, but it's too focused on the waffle.

My food's starting to get cold now, but the canary has my full attention. Sometimes I'd watch you just the same. You'd be reading, or watching television, and when I should have been doing something else, I'd lose track of my responsibilities and just watch.

The canary finishes the waffle and hops to its perch on the chair. The wind picks up, and the rain soaks my back, so I lean forward a little. The canary misconstrues my movement and flies off into the rain, yellow eventually disappearing in gray.

Others

Amelia Earhart assumed the identity of Irene Bolam, and she (Amelia) vanished from the public eye, even when she (Irene) did not.

There are no eyewitness accounts of John Haster de-planing. Fans of his work have put his "ten clues" rule to the test, but they've never added up.

Frederick Valentich encountered an unidentified craft flying at high speed dangerously close to his Cessna.

What's most striking about Ambrose Bierce is his story "The Difficulties of Crossing a Field," in which a man vanishes walking a field, which seems to predict his own fate.

The Norfolk Regiment marched into a mist, then the mist seemed to rise, vertically, and joined the rest of the clouds in the sky.

Glenn Miller never made it across the English Channel.

David Lang was a hoax based on "The Difficulties of Crossing a Field."

The crew and passengers of the Joyita in the South Pacific. Five weeks later, the Joyita returned with no one on board.

The Flannery Isle lighthouse keepers, from their stations, leaving behind equipment important to surviving the hostile conditions at that location and time of year.

The Kelpie, once harnessed or mounted, leaps into the nearest body of water, taking its human captor with it.

New Hampshire's Old Man on the Mountain, on a foggy day.

You, me, and everyone else, if it makes it all easier to swallow.

Number Eight

Found the rock again, but it's not spinning. How has it changed? What is the season? There are shavings in my mouth. Will they be of any greater value in my ears, pockets, or over my eyes, combined with the rock? It sings music, sweats motion, teeters on the brink of immolation, and even so, it may not be a rock, could be a seed, could be the reason it doesn't spin. The difference may be key, but don't discount the effect of commonality.

Your Grandmother's Transformation

Your grandmother has transformed from living, geriatric being to corpse, to cadaver, to decaying flesh underground, and will eventually become bones only. Bones some day decompose to a fine dust. The cheap box housing her will also break apart, and she will be absorbed by the earth. At which point has she disappeared? Is disappearance actually possible?

A Maze as a Map

We took an aerial shot of the maze, printed it, and used it
for a map. Made lines that zigzagged from start to finish
with pink fluorescent highlighter. The walls of corn seven
feet tall, five feet thick, covering six acres. Exit and entrance
are only separated by five feet. So, we're going to spend
hours in this thing, and we're only going five feet to the left?
I say. You ignore me and enter.

We make a left turn. Inside the maze, surrounded by
nothing but stalks of corn, with no points of reference, the
map was useless, and you knew it would be, so you
memorized your turns. Left, pass opening on left, pass
opening on right, next right, next left. You're only a few feet
ahead, but I lose you around every turn. I make the turn
and find you, just for a second before you disappear behind
another turn. Left, pass two more lefts, left, quick left,

immediate right.

I make the next left, but don't see you. Right, right, pass right, pass left, u-turn on right, left, instead of right, right, second right, left. If we took that aerial shot of the maze right now, it would show us separated by only a few walls of corn. I the brown dot, you the yellow. Left, right, straight past four openings, next left, all in vain, no hope of catching up to you. I stand still to listen, but now we're too far apart for sound to give any indication of where you might be. Everything I've learned about being lost is to stay put, wait for help, but that's not what I do.

I run straight through the corn walls, knowing I'll eventually make it out. I hold up my arms to block my face, but ears of corn still slap me, husks still cut me. After several minutes of small cuts on the back on my hands and cornsilk in my eyes, mouth, hair, I emerge from the maze five feet from the exit, but on the side opposite the entrance. Now I sit and wait, but you don't appear. It's been hours and you're still not out. The aerial shot shows the brown dot outside the maze, but no yellow inside.

City Lights

When all the lights in the city go out, and I no longer see, it disappears from my view, but not altogether. Still there, people still existing, but shifting always, inhabiting different, sometimes darker spaces. When the lights go back on, the city, the people don't change, the shift of disappearance and reappearance externally manifest. Physicality continues even if visuality does not.

We Taste the Wetness Together

You live in a hole.

For thirty minutes a day, as the sun drifts by overhead,
light filters through the dense foliage of the surrounding
Xetl trees and you can see.

Every few days, roots puncture the walls of your hole.
You nestle your cheek against the soil and gnaw on the
root. Otherwise, you eat soil dense with nutrients and
moisture.

The dirt under your fingernails and in the cracks of
your skin is permanent now.

When animals fall into your hole, don't eat them. Let

them reside for a time, then help them free.

Open your mouth when it rains, but when it fills the hole to your neck, close it.

Clothes never dry, but moisture recedes into soil.

Your hole is a cylinder, eight feet deep, three in diameter.

Over time, you acquire a taste for soil only, but don't neglect the roots. Neglected roots form a ladder system, and you may be tempted to climb out, but you won't have to resist for long. It only lasts a few minutes; then you appreciate the roots.

One week out of the year, the Xetl tree drops foliage. Stockpile as much as falls in your hole for padding and warmth, but don't eat the leaves.

I'm in the hole with you. Not for help or comfort, but for a shared experience.

When you open your mouth in the rain, I open mine. We can taste the wetness at the same time, but not together. When cold, I can be cold too. Experience it together, but never discuss it.

Number Nine

They're all useless all, the search futile, the numbers a waste of yours and mine. What have I missed? What is missing? Is there anything to miss? We watch together, you and I, complicit in what happens. Despite the distance we try to forge between us, we still remain linked in this one act, you a participant now. If I saw you walking like I used to, you would see it, you would watch it all the same. The difference is you watch me too. I talk to you, you not to me, but I'm counting on your perspective, banking on your ability to reason. What I miss, you miss, and what you miss, I never get a sense of.

You in the Flood

It happens like this. I make it through the day usually, up to the point where I'm lying in bed with dog pelts, and I've stopped distracting myself with periphery. It comes in a flood. You in the flood. It starts with images, usually of you walking. At first in the rain, then snow, eventually sun, all days compounded into one disorderly sequence of images. Quick and seemingly random, then slow and repeating. As the images slow, fragments of conversations loop. Sometimes image and audio align, but it's not a sure bet, and it's easier when they don't. Eventually, I have to get up. Crawl out of bed, slip on socks, slide across the hardwood, down the stairs. In the kitchen, I open the pantry, reach in the back for a small bag. The seeds I want are in the bag, at least a hundred in there, but I only take out five. Sitting at the table, seeds lined up in front of me, with a glass of water. Pop one seed in, wait thirty minutes, then pop another. Between seeds, I go back to my bed and get the dog pelts, and then, seated in the kitchen, set them at my feet. Swallow another seed. Repeat until gone. Wait to see if they'll work tonight.

The Surface of Motion

Did she exist? A passenger I can no longer describe or account for? There was an absence there, but one so constant it became familiar. Each time I see her, I think about the white path, beyond the color of fields, heat, appearing in moments of tranquility. She is there, she is always there, appearing voiceless, faceless, terraced, among trees, renewed through the act of memory. All my ideas are liquid, and there is water where memory should be.

The Seed of the Xetl Tree

The muscles in her face slide down off the bone and rest in her neck. The subcutaneous fat rests slightly higher in her jowls.

The seed of the Xetl tree may be implanted orally or vaginally. In either method, iron is key to germination. In the vaginal method, the seed is implanted in the uterine wall, generally around the time of ovulation, and absorbs iron from the endometrial layer. When taken orally, the seed enters the stomach and, in best cases, attaches to the upper stomach and absorbs iron as nutrients pass through the stomach lining. Most often, the seed of the Xetl tree drops into the pool of stomach acid and disintegrates.

She holds a small mug full of green tea in her only hand, takes a sip, and throws the mug against the wall. She tries to scream, but it comes out as muffled sound because she no longer has the facial muscles required to move her jaw. The mug chips on the rim, but otherwise sits intact on the floor. The steaming water collects in a spreading pool, with tea leaves clumped in the middle. She rubs her nub arm on her thigh.

A week ago she called me.

> Will you help me with something?
> Should be able to, but depends.
> On what? Why won't you just help?
> Depends on what it is and how much it'll cost

me. She hung up. Five minutes later, called back. I need help getting something and it won't cost you anything.

The oral method has a higher failure rate, but works more efficiently when successful. The higher failure rate often requires multiple attempts at implantation.

When implanted vaginally, the seed of the Xetl tree has a failure rate nearing zero but takes much longer to germinate.

My phone rings. Hello? On the other end, an unintelligible reply. I'll come over, I say.

The successful vaginal attempt will take at least a week to germinate because it is necessary for the endometrial layer to thicken around the seed. Once germination occurs, the seed of the Xetl tree is impervious to menstrual flushing.

It is recommended to wait several days between attempts at oral implantation. The successful attempt will usually manifest itself within hours, but can take up to a full day, depending on diet. Fragments of the unsuccessful seed do not get absorbed into the body. It is therefore necessary to wait until seed matter is excreted through fecal matter.

A seed of the Xetl tree clings to her uterine wall as the endometrium thickens around it.

She pops the seed I just brought her into her mouth, and washes it down with wheat grass. Now we wait, I say. She nods until the fat in her jowls and the muscles in her neck offer resistance. She motions with her arm for me to sit beside her. The fat under her arm continues to wave after the rest of her arm has stopped. The seed attaches itself to her stomach lining and absorbs iron from the wheat grass. Following germination, the seed of the Xetl tree will pierce the stomach or uterine lining and spread tendrils throughout the body along vein and artery paths. These tendrils are as soft and flexible as the veins and arteries themselves. Whereas the seed of the Xetl tree absorbs iron, the tendrils draw toxins out of surrounding tissue. The toxin absorption process allows the tendrils to continue growth in both circumference and length, but also frees the body of destructive substances.

The tendrils in her arm expand, extend to the end of her nub arm, push the skin until they form a hand and fingers. Tendrils of the Xetl tree absorb excess fat from her arms, thighs, ass, torso, neck, and burn it for energy. They push the muscles back up into her face. She smiles.

You're back, I say.

Get me a mirror, please.

I run to the bathroom, rip the mirror off the wall, struggle to carry it to her. She stares at her reflection.

You

No, wait, she says and continues to stare for several minutes. I'm beautiful. She leaves the room briefly, returns with a camera. Here, she says and hands it to me. Take my picture.

She sits at home, holding the picture in her new hand. The seed of the Xetl tree, deep in the iron rich endometrial layer, sprouts and pierces the uterine wall, spreads throughout her body.

What's wrong, I say. She's in pain and can't speak, so she screams into the phone. I'm coming over.

She waits in the front yard, standing calmly, perhaps confused, belying her demeanor on the phone. As I approach, tendrils puncture the end of her toes and burrow into the ground. Her body stiffens as tendrils double up on existing paths. They feed off nutrients from her body, suck bones of marrow and veins of blood, replace blood with plant matter, and eventually form a solid mass just below her sternum that spreads vertically in both directions. I watch as the mass shoots downward through her vagina into the ground, forming a deep, intricate root system. Her head thrusts up as the mass moves through her chest to her neck, mouth wide open as it moves through her windpipe, and as she gasps for air, the trunk of the Xetl tree exits her gaping mouth, slowly at first, then building speed as it sucks in carbon dioxide through it's emerging foliage. It absorbs her, expands upward and outward, until she is a Xetl tree, firmly rooted in her front lawn.

Made in the USA
Charleston, SC
25 February 2010